The Great CHRISTIAN DECEPTION

BY ERNIE HASLER, SCOTTISH WRITER

InfusedMedia Co. LLC
www.infusedmedia.co
1-888-251-6088

Books of the Bible – A brief, focused, synopsis by Ernie Hasler to help us put the Bible into perspective.

Introduction: Most people do not believe in Yahweh (The Creator and Sustainer God); they usually, blindly, follow their dominant parent living in communities controlled by particular **sun-worshipping religious traditions.**

A social, political, hierarchy.

Most modern Bibles are corrupted.

The Creator Elohim's (God's) **Sacred Name** was removed under the pressure of **Hellenisation**.

Like the modern world, the Greeks of that time hated anything Jewish. Under fear of persecution, torture and death, the Jews replaced **Yahweh's** name in what is wrongly called The Old Testament, with the **Sun God Baal's**, title **Lord**.

Jews later constructed the excuse that they removed his name to protect people from breaking the Third Commandment: **"Thou shalt not take the Name of Yahweh Elohim in vain!"** But that was just guilty justification.

In a similar vein, the Pagan writers of what is erroneously called, The New Testament, changed the name **Yeshua** (meaning salvation) the Messiah, to variations of Ieous Horus Krishna, three major idol gods of the Roman Empire.

Centuries later, when the letter J was introduced into some languages, this name shortened to Jesus Christ.

(Christ being Sanskrit for Kristina, Sanskrit is the classical language of India and the liturgical language of Hinduism, Buddhism, and Jainism.

The name Sanskrit means "refined", "consecrated" and "sanctified".) (Krishna, Sanskrit Kṛṣṇa (O Lord Kṛṣṇa) one of the most widely revered and popular of all Indian divinities, worshipped as the eighth incarnation (avatar) of the Hindu god Vishnu and also as a supreme idol god in his own right.

Emperor Constantine commissioned this name, Leous Horus Krishna and the writing of the so-called, **New Testament** in 325 A.D. To **create** a universal god and religion for what he saw as his universal Empire.

'A universal Church for a universal Empire'.

Let's examine the Bible to see if there is a common theme?

Genesis Summary — Like it's meaning, Genesis is the book of beginnings, starting so long ago as time began.

The Creation story, a simple metaphor for enormous and complex happenings, over much time.

(Scientists cannot reach back to the beginning or explain what caused **Creation**, especially where all this stuff came from, we can only see a small part of the total, most of it is made up of Dark Matter and Dark Energy and we as individuals cannot envisage how much stuff there is in the universe.

The story is a simple metaphor of creation then the beginnings of human history (the universe, earth and man), humanity's fall from grace, the story of Noah's flood and the tower of Babel.

The story of the Tower of Babel is about the origins of the multiplicity of languages. Yahweh was concerned that humans had blasphemed by building the tower to avoid a second flood, so to slow their progress, Yahweh brought into existence multiple languages. Thus, humans were divided into linguistic groups, unable to understand one another.

Genesis also tells the story of Yahweh's long and patient plan to **redeem** both man and the world, beginning with a covenant with Abraham.

(could this be the Bible's common theme?)

The rest of Genesis tells of the lives of the patriarchs Abraham, Isaac, Jacob and Joseph, leading to the descendants of these patriarchs, blessed through Joseph by Yahweh, whose people were now living in Egypt.

***Exodus* Summary**—A new harder Pharaoh enslaves the Hebrew people of Yahweh, who in their pain and misery, cry out to Yahweh for deliverance.

Yahweh raises up Moses, through whom he delivers his people from Pharaoh, through a series of natural plagues.

Exodus 3:13-15

13 Then Moses replied to Elohim, "Suppose I go to the people of Israel and say to them, 'The Elohim of your ancestors has sent me to you,' and they ask me, 'What is his name?' What should I tell them?"

14 Elohim answered Moses, **"Ehyeh Who Ehyeh. This is what you must say to the people of Israel: 'Ehyeh has sent me to you.'"**

15 Again Elohim said to Moses, "This is what you must say to the people of Israel: **Yahweh Elohim** of your ancestors, the Elohim of Abraham, Isaac, and Jacob, has sent me to you. **This is my name forever. This is my title throughout every generation.**

Yahweh then guides his people to Mount Sinai where he gives them a set of laws, a constitution by which to live.

The people of Yahweh become the nation of Yahweh now called **Israel.**

The Ten Commandments are part of that law and represent the whole law's essence.

Yahweh orders the building of his tabernacle so that he can (**figuratively**) dwell amongst his people.

Leviticus Summary—Yahweh gives more laws to his people through Moses, governing their sacrifices and festivals.

In addition, Yahweh gives **an essential set of purity laws** to his people, including dietary restrictions to keep them holy. (the word holy here, means identifying with Yahweh, or belonging to him). For example. Pig meat in itself is not unclean. (Antiochus IV (Epiphanes), the king of Syria, captured Jerusalem in 167 BC and desecrated the Temple by offering the sacrifice of a pig **on an altar to Zeus** (the Abomination of Desolation). (That is what makes pig meat unclean).

Numbers Summary—Due to false reporting, Israel lacks faith in entering the Promised Land. Yahweh punishes Israel by making them wander in the desert for forty years, staying in Sukkot's (dismantlable tent-like dwellings), until all of the adult generations that came out of Egypt has died. *(The Feast of Sukkot, or Tabernacles, **one of Yahweh's appointed times Leviticus 23,** remembers this time by living in a temporary dwelling during the autumn time of Sukkot, I like the name Tabernacles, I can envisage a temporary tent-like dwelling).*

The true origon of the name for the **Scoti or Scotii**, derived from the name Sukkots.

However, the modern world thinks the word "Scot" is found in Latin texts from the fourth century describing a tribe which sailed from Ireland to raid Roman Britain.

Yes, this is also true, but it does not know of our ancient origins and forty years in the wilderness.

The book of Numbers takes its name from the census that is conducted at the beginning of the book to count the number of men in order to determine the size of Yahweh's army that would have conquered the Promised Land.

Modern scholars say this was 5,500, not 603,550, as in the Bible

Deuteronomy Summary—"Deuteronomy" means "the second law", it is a renewal of the laws that Yahweh previously gave to his people at Mount Sinai. *The reason the laws are repeated is that the adult generation that came out of Egypt has passed away and a new generation must renew their covenant with Yahweh, just like we must renew our covenant with Yahweh.* ***A test for us is; do we keep his appointed times?****(see Leviticus 23)*

Deuteronomy 4:30 "When you are in distress and all these things have come upon you, in the latter days you will return to Yahweh your Elohim and listen to His voice.

Deuteronomy 30:2 "and you return to the LORD your God and obey Him with all your heart and soul according to all that I command you today, you and your sons,

Leviticus 23

1. (1-3) **The Sabbath.**

And Yahweh spoke to Moses, saying, "Speak to the children of Israel and say to them: 'The feasts of Yahweh, which you shall proclaim to be holy convocations, these are My feasts. 'Six days shall work be done, but the seventh day is a Sabbath of solemn rest, a holy convocation. You shall do no work on it; it is the Sabbath of Yahweh in all your dwellings. *Saturday is the seventh day of the week starting Friday sunset, ending Saturday sunset.*

    a. The feasts of Yahweh: This chapter introduces us to the seven annual feasts Israel celebrated. These feasts are rich with **symbolic and prophetic significance.**

    b. The seventh day is a Sabbath of solemn rest: The weekly Sabbath was not properly a feast, but similar to the feast days, **it was a day set apart unto Yahweh**, and so a reminder regarding the Sabbath is included here.

2. (4-5) **The feast of Passover**.

'These are the feasts of Yahweh, holy convocations which you shall proclaim at their appointed times. *You need a Hebrew to the Gregorian calendar converter.* On the fourteenth day of the first Hebrew month at twilight is Yahweh's Passover.

   a. On the fourteenth day of the first Hebrew month: On the Jewish ceremonial calendar, the first Hebrew month was known as Nisan; Passover was held on the fourteenth of Nisan each year.

   b. Yahweh's Passover: Passover was meant to commemorate Israel's deliverance from Egypt, and with the sacrifice of the lamb for each family, show how the blood of the lamb averted the judgment of Yahweh for each Israelite family.

3. (6-8) **The feast of Unleavened Bread.**

And on the fifteenth day of the same Hebrew month is the Feast of Unleavened Bread to Yahweh; seven days you must eat unleavened bread. On the first day, you shall have a holy convocation; you shall do no customary work on it. But you shall offer an offering made by fire to Yahweh for seven days. The seventh day shall be a holy convocation; you shall do no customary work on it.'"

   a. The Feast of Unleavened Bread to Yahweh: The feast of unleavened bread was a week-long celebration the week immediately following Passover (from Nisan 15 to Nisan 21). This feast showed the purity

Israel was to walk in (illustrated by eating only bread without leaven, a type of sin) after the blood-deliverance of Passover.

4. (9-14) **The Feast of Firstfruits.**

And Yahweh spoke to Moses, saying, "Speak to the children of Israel and say to them: 'When you come into the land which I give to you, and reap its harvest, then you shall bring a sheaf of the firstfruits of your harvest to the priest. He shall wave the sheaf before YAHWEH, to be accepted on your behalf; on the day after the Sabbath the priest shall wave it.

And you shall offer on that day, when you wave the sheaf, a male lamb of the first year, without blemish, as a burnt offering to Yahweh.

Its grain offering shall be two-tenths of an ephah of fine flour mixed with oil, an offering made by fire to Yahweh, for a sweet aroma; and its drink offering shall be of wine, one-fourth of a hin. You shall eat neither bread nor parched grain nor fresh grain until the same day that you have brought an offering to your Yahweh; **it shall be a statute forever throughout your generations in all your dwellings.**

   a. Then you shall bring a sheaf of the firstfruits of your harvest to the priest: The day following Passover's Sabbath was a time to give the firstfruits of the harvest to Yahweh. The idea was to dedicate the first ripened stalks of grain to Yahweh, in anticipation of a greater harvest to come.

b. "The firstfruits at Passover would be barley, which ripens in the warmer areas as early as March."

5. (15-21) **The feast of Pentecost** (also called the Feast of Weeks).

'And you shall count for yourselves from the day after the Sabbath, from the day that you brought the sheaf of the wave offering: seven Sabbaths shall be completed. Count fifty days to the day after the seventh Sabbath; then you shall offer a new grain offering to Yahweh. You shall bring from your dwellings two wave loaves of two-tenths of an ephah. They shall be of fine flour; they shall be baked with leaven. They are the firstfruits to Yahweh. And you shall offer with the bread seven lambs of the first year, without blemish, one young bull, and two rams.

They shall be as a burnt offering to Yahweh, with their grain offering and their drink offerings, an offering made by fire for a sweet aroma to Yahweh. Then you shall sacrifice one kid of the goats as a sin offering, and two male lambs of the first year as a sacrifice of a peace offering. The priest shall wave them with the bread of the firstfruits as a wave offering before Yahweh, with the two lambs. They shall be holy to Yahweh for the priest.

And you shall proclaim on the same day that it is a holy convocation to you. You shall do no customary work on it. **It shall be a statute forever in all your dwellings throughout your generations.**

a. Count fifty days to the day after the seventh Sabbath; then you shall offer a new grain offering to Yahweh: Fifty days after the feast of firstfruits, at the completion of the wheat harvest, Israel was to celebrate the Feast of Pentecost by bringing a new grain offering to Yahweh; and by waving two loaves of leavened bread unto Yahweh.

6. (22) **Generosity to the poor and stranger.**

'When you reap the harvest of your land, you shall not wholly reap the corners of your field when you reap, nor shall you gather any gleaning from your harvest. You shall leave them for the poor and for the stranger: I am Yahweh your Yahweh.'"

    a. You shall not wholly reap the corners of your field when you reap: This repeats the command of Leviticus 19:9-10; this was a law to provide a means for the poor and the stranger to eat by working for themselves and gleaning what was left behind. This was an appropriate reminder right after the law concerning the harvest feast of Pentecost.

7. (23-25) **The feast of Trumpets** (Rosh Hashanah).

Then Yahweh spoke to Moses, saying, "Speak to the children of Israel, saying: 'In the seventh Hebrew month, on the first day of the Hebrew month, you shall have a sabbath-rest, a memorial of blowing of trumpets, a holy convocation. You shall do no customary work on it, and you shall offer an offering made by fire to Yahweh.'"

    a. *A memorial of blowing of trumpets, a holy convocation: On the first day of the Hebrew month*

b. *Yeshua continued in Matthew 24:29: "Immediately
after the tribulation of those days the sun will be
darkened, and the moon will not give its light; the
stars will fall from heaven, and the powers of the
heavens will be shaken."*

c. *He said that all nations on earth would see the sign
of His coming and would mourn. Then He stated
that they would see Him coming with power and
glory and that He would send His angels to gather
His resurrected followers with **a great sound of a
trumpet** (Matthew 24:30-31).*

8. (26-32) **The Day of Atonement** (Yom Kippur).

And YAHWEH spoke to Moses, saying: "Also the tenth
day of this seventh Hebrew month shall be the Day of
Atonement. It shall be a holy convocation for you; you
shall afflict your souls, and offer an offering made by fire
to YAHWEH. And you shall do no work on that same day,
for it is the Day of Atonement, to make atonement for you
before YAHWEH your Yahweh. For any person who is not
afflicted in soul on that same day shall be cut off from his
people. And any person who does any work on that same
day, that person I will destroy from among his people.

You shall do no manner of work; it shall be a statute
forever throughout your generations in all your dwellings.
It shall be to you a sabbath of solemn rest, and you shall

afflict your souls; on the ninth day of the Hebrew month at evening, from evening to evening, you shall celebrate your sabbath."

    a. Also, the tenth day of this seventh Hebrew month shall be the Day of Atonement: On the tenth of Tishri, the people gathered again for a holy convocation; but this was not a celebration feast, but a day to afflict your souls in humble recognition of one's sin and need for atonement.

    b. And you shall afflict your souls: The specific priestly procedures for the Day of Atonement were described in Leviticus 16. This passage records the command for the people of Israel to set that day aside as a solemn day of reflection.

The Feast of Tabernacles (Succoth).

Then YAHWEH spoke to Moses, saying, "Speak to the children of Israel, saying: 'The fifteenth day of this seventh Hebrew month shall be the Feast of Tabernacles for seven days to YAHWEH. On the first day, there shall be a holy convocation. You shall do no customary work on it. For seven days you shall offer an offering made by fire to YAHWEH.

The Great Last Day (eighth day)

On the eighth day, you shall have a holy convocation, and you shall offer an offering made by fire to YAHWEH. It is a sacred assembly, and you shall do no customary work on it.

So Moses declared to the children of Israel the feasts of YAHWEH.

Joshua Summary—After Israel's renewal of the covenant in Deuteronomy (just before entering the promised land), the Book of Joshua narrates the conquest of this land and the division of the land among the twelve tribes of Israel.

Judges Summary—After Joshua's death, the people of Yahweh drift into a cycle of sin which included: idolatry, the judgment of Yahweh by an invading army, the people's repentance and clamour for deliverance, raising of a judge and the peace of Yahweh's people.

This cycle repeats itself no fewer than twelve times in the Book of Judges. (Yes, that's us, repeatedly unfaithful whores.)

Ruth—Occurring during the time of the judges, this book tells the story of a foreigner (**an immigrant**) called Ruth who's name means friend, who becomes part of Yahweh's people through marriage.

(Good news for all those who wish to become part of Spiritual Israel).

A famine has destroyed the farm of Elimelech of Bethlehem, driving him and his wife Naomi to the land of Moab. There, with the help of their two sons, they do well for a time, and the sons marry Gentile women of the region, Orpah, and the good and beautiful Ruth, a Moabite.

But tragedy strikes the family once again. Ruth, a woman who after being widowed remains with her husband's mother. ...**Key verse:** Ruth 1:14 But Ruth answered, "Don't force me to leave you. Don't make me turn back from following you. Wherever you go, I will go, and wherever you stay, I will stay. Your people will be my people, **and your Elohim will be my Elohim.**

Ruth accompanies Naomi to Bethlehem and later marries Boaz, a distant relative of her late father-in-law. She is a symbol of abiding loyalty and devotion. Boaz noticed Ruth, the widowed Moabite daughter-in-law of Naomi, a relative of his, gleaning grain in his fields. ... In marrying Ruth, Boaz revives Elimelech's lineage, and the patrimony is secured to Naomi's family. Their son was Obed, father of Jesse, and grandfather of David and so on, **a bloodline directly to Yeshua the Messiah.**

1 and 2 Samuel Summary—Tells of the establishment of the ministry of the prophet Samuel who anoints Saul as the first king of Israel and is witness to the rise of the united kingdom in Israel. These books then trace Saul's demise and David's ascendance and kingship.

1 Samuel 7:3 "Then Samuel spoke to all the house of Israel, saying, "**If you return to Yahweh** with all your heart, remove the foreign gods and the Ashtaroth from among you and direct your hearts to the LORD and serve Him alone; and He will deliver you from the hand of the Philistines."

1 and 2 Kings Summary—Narrates Solomon's kingship, the divided kingdom of Israel and Judah, and Yahweh's judgment of his disobedient people into exile.

1 and 2 Chronicles Summary—First and Second Chronicles is that history for Israel. It's the story of Israel's kings and God's faithfulness to His promises. Tells of David and Solomon's kingship as well as a selection of southern kings and Judah's judgment into exile. First and Second Chronicles is written for the people who returned from exile as a way to encourage them in their faith.

They were spiritual heirs of David and Solomon and Yahweh would not forget the promises he made to David and to his people. Thus, David and Solomon are portrayed in a more positive light, and only the southern kingdom (Judah) is highlighted.

The books of Chronicles are long. They're full of genealogies and records. But they're the records of Yahweh's long-lasting faithfulness to His people, even when they are not faithful to Him.

2 Chronicles 15:4 "But in their distress, **they turned to Yahweh the Elohim of Israel, and they sought Him, and He let them find Him.**

Ezra and Nehemiah Summary—These two books should be seen as one volume. They narrate the return of the exiles from Babylon in three different groups. One is led by Zerubbabel, who begins to rebuild the temple. Another is led by Nehemiah, who rebuilds the walls of Jerusalem. A third is led by Ezra the scribe, who teaches Yahweh's people the law and reestablishes the worship of Yahweh and Israel's festivals.

Nehemiah 1:9 but if you return to Me and keep My commandments and do them, though those of you who have been scattered were in the most remote part of the heavens, I will gather them from there and will bring them to the place where I have chosen to cause My name to dwell.'

Ezra and Nehemiah overcame obstacle after obstacle finishing the missions that Yahweh had given them. Because of the strong commitment of these three men, Yahweh saved the Jewish people from captivity in Babylon and restored their city in Jerusalem.

Esther Summary—Occurs during the exile of Israel and retells the story of Queen Esther, a Jew who saves her people from an evil plot to destroy them.

Esther, the beautiful Jewish wife of the Persian king Ahasuerus (Xerxes I), and her cousin Mordecai persuade the king to retract an order for the general annihilation of Jews throughout the empire. The massacre had been plotted by the king's chief minister, Haman, and the date decided by casting lots (Purim).

The theme of the book of Esther is Yahweh's protection of Israel. **Although Yahweh is actually not mentioned in the book,** He clearly saves His people from the scheme of Haman. Throughout history, the Jewish people have been treated unjustly, and the story of Esther tells of one of those occurrences.

Job Summary—The Book of Job. The story is a test of Job's faith by removing everything that is of value to him (wealth, family and health).

It is a conversation between Job and his three friends who argue about why Job is suffering and conclude that it is due to sin in Job's life. Job defends his innocence before his friends.

Elihu enters the picture and suggests to Job that he needs to be more humble since Yahweh is not required to explain himself.

Yahweh finally answers Job but offers no explanation for the suffering.

Instead, Yahweh humbles Job and seeks to remove any sense of self-righteousness in order that he might find his purpose in Yahweh. The book ends with Yahweh restoring some of the things Job had lost.

Job 22:23 "If you return to the Almighty, you will be restored; If you remove unrighteousness far from your tent.

Psalms Summary—The Book of Psalms is a hymnbook for the Hebrew nation. It contains 150 songs and prayers that focus on Israel's religious life. 70 Psalms are attributed to King David.

There are different types of Psalms: Laments / praises; royal Psalms (where Yahweh's kingship is celebrated); thanksgiving Psalms; and interestingly, **Messianic Psalms** that the New Testament writers used in speaking about Yeshua (for example Psalm 22).

One of the most beloved parts of Scripture is Psalm 23 while Psalm 119 celebrates the goodness of Yahweh's word. It is also the longest Psalm.

Proverbs Summary—Proverbs are short sayings about a moral truth or principle. The Book of Proverbs is to teach wisdom for Yahweh living, wisdom that originates and comes from Yahweh.

Wisdom is more precious than gold and only a fool is not interested in receiving its instructions.

Ecclesiastes Summary—The Book of Ecclesiastes is attributed to Solomon and is a biography that examines the meaning of life. One of his conclusions is that all of man's actions are essentially transitory, meaningless and vanity where death is inevitable. Therefore one should enjoy life's simple pleasures including work which is Yahweh's gift to humans. His final charge to us is: **Fear Yahweh and keep his commandment for that is the whole duty of everyone.** (Eccl 12:13).

Song of Solomon Summary—An explicit love poem that depicts the ideal love that should exist between a man and a woman in marriage. *Verse 5. I rose up to open for my beloved. My hands dripped with myrrh, my fingers with liquid myrrh, on the handles of the lock. My fingers with liquid myrrh. In the night, her fingers were dripping with liquid myrrh. She clearly had been masturbating in hopeful* *anticipation,* ***it is not written in condemnation, but a true reflection on life.***

This song celebrates intimacy, sexual desire and the marital love of man to woman and woman to man.

The song also serves as a metaphor for the covenant love that exists between Yahweh and his people (and possibly all life). Indeed, faithful marriage is the proper picture that models our relationship with Yahweh.

Isaiah Summary (so much to try to summerise)

1-12 – Jerusalem judged and redeemed

13-27 – Yahweh's righteousness established among the nations.

13-23 features burdens and judgments largely, though there are some words of comfort, eg, in the image of the key of David at the end of chapter 22.

24-27, sometimes called the 'mini-apocalypse' **sees Yahweh's righteous judgment more broadly in terms of His victory over death, and the rising of the dead.**

In Isaiah 26:19 it says: **But your dead will live, Yahweh; their bodies will rise—**

28-35 – **the coming of a righteous king in Jerusalem - Yahweh sends the prophet Isaiah to warn Israel of future judgment—but also to tell them about a**

coming king and servant who will "bear the sins of many."

36-39 – Jerusalem saved (from Sennacherib), but the shadow of Babylon looms (after Hezekiah shows the treasury to Babylonian ambassadors)

40-55 – the return to Jerusalem from Babylonian captivity

56-66 – new heavens and a new earth. Even in the new Zion, however, there are suggestions that there will be some backsliding and merely perfunctory worship (eg chapter 48; 65:11-12).

Isaiah 31:6 "Return to Him from whom you have deeply defected, O sons of Israel".

Isaiah 10:21 "A remnant will return, the remnant of Jacob, to the mighty Elohim.

Isaiah 19:22 "Yahweh will strike Egypt, striking but healing; so they will return to Yahweh, and He will respond to them and will heal them.

Isaiah 55:7 "Let the wicked forsake his way And the unrighteous man his thoughts; **And let him return to Yahweh our Elohim**, And He will have compassion on him, And to our Elohim, For He will abundantly pardon".

Isaiah 59:20 "A Redeemer will come to Zion, And to those who turn from transgression in Jacob," declares Yahweh. (Jacob are the ten lost tribes scattered throughout the world).

Yahweh is called 'the Holy One of Israel' over twenty times in Isaiah.

Jeremiah

Yahweh sends a prophet to warn Israel about the coming Babylonian captivity, but the people don't take the news very well.

1 – the call of Jeremiah

2-6 – poetic pronouncements of judgment and calls to repent

7-10 – the people's falseness in worship

11-20 – falseness in the covenant, and the people's sin

21-24 – the failure of Judah's kings and prophets

25 – Yahweh's judgment on all nations by Babylon, and Babylon judged in turn

26-29 – Babylonian supremacy is foretold

30-33 – 'the Book of Consolation', containing a promise that Judah and Israel will be restored. **The phrase 'I will bring you back from captivity' occurs six times.** There will be a *new* covenant (not a renewed one in the vain of Joshua or Josiah), which will include both Israel and Judah.

34-36 – king and people reject the word of Jeremiah; Jehoiakim burns Jeremiah's scroll.

37-39 – Judah falls

40-45 – the fate of those who were left; the assassination of Gedaliah and the flight into Egypt

46-51 – the oracles against the nations

52 – further account of the fall of Jerusalem, and the destruction of the temple

Jeremiah 4:1 "If you will return, O Israel," declares Yahweh, "Then you should return to Me And if you will put away your detested things from My presence, And will not waver.

Jeremiah 24:7 'I will give them a heart to know Me, for I am Yahweh their Elohim; and they will be My people, and I will be their Elohim, **for they will return to Me with their whole heart.**

Jeremiah 3:12

"Go and proclaim these words toward the north and say, **'Return faithless Israel,' declares Yahweh;** 'I will not look upon you in anger For I am gracious,' declares Yahweh; 'I will not be angry forever.

Jeremiah 3:14 'Return, O faithless sons,' declares Yahweh; 'For I am a master to you, And I will take you one from a city and two from a family, And I will bring you to Zion.'

Jeremiah 3:22 "Return, O faithless sons, I will heal your faithlessness." "Behold, we come to You; For You are Yahweh our Elohim.

Jeremiah 15:19 "Therefore, thus says Yahweh, "If you return, then I will restore you-- Before Me, you will stand; And if you extract the precious from the worthless, You will become My spokesman. They for their part may turn to you, But as for you, you must not turn to them.

Lamentations

A collection of dirges lamenting the fall of Jerusalem after the Babylonian attacks.

How doth the city sit solitary, that was full of people! The city is a widow. Desolate. Beauty has departed from the daughter of Zion.

Her nakedness has been seen, and she, therefore, courts dishonour.

Behold, and see if there be any sorrow like unto my sorrow. The daughter of Judah is crushed as in a wine press.

Lamentation of sin expressed in the first person. The daughter of Zion is covered with the cloud of Yahweh's anger.

Yahweh has been pitiless.

He has burned against Judah like a flaming fire.

Yahweh is now an enemy.

He has taken away his tabernacle, ie, his presence has departed.

Feasts and Sabbaths are forgotten in Zion. *(as they are in Christianity)*

The elders are girded with sackcloth casting dust on their heads.

Enemies hiss and gnash. Arise in the night and pour out thine heart like water. Virgins and young men are dead by the sword. I am the man that hath seen affliction by the rod of his wrath.

Yahweh has brought me into darkness and old age.

My prayers are shut out.

Yahweh attacks with a bow, breaking teeth; Yahweh is compared to a bear or a lion. However, Yahweh has stopped short of complete destruction.

Yahweh will not cast off forever. The author models the repentance he deems appropriate and prays for vengeance on his enemies. Gold has become dim.

Children lack bread.

The iniquity of the daughter of my people is greater than the punishment of the sin of Sodom.

Those not slain by the sword die lingeringly of hunger.

The Nazarites have gone from being purer than snow to having visages blacker than coal.

*****John the Baptist and Yeshua were Nazarites, teachers and protectors of Torah.*****

The ruin of the exultant Edomites is predicted – there is an ironic invitation for Edom to rejoice, drink and be naked.

The punishment of Zion is accomplished (ie completed). Yahweh is invited to remember the reproaches that Judah has borne.

The people have been humiliated, and dancing has turned to mourning.

Yahweh, however, remains forever.

Turn unto us – but thou hast utterly rejected us; thou art very wroth against us.

Lamentations 3:40 "Let us examine and probe our ways, **And let us return to Yahweh our Elohim**".

Yahweh chooses a man to speak for Him to Israel, to tell them the error of their ways and teach them justice:

Ezekiel.

Ezekiel's early oracles (from c. 592) in Jerusalem were pronouncements of violence and destruction; his later statements addressed the hopes of the Israelites exiled in Babylon.

The faith of Ezekiel in the ultimate establishment of a new covenant between Yahweh and the people of Israel has had a profound influence on the postexilic reconstruction and reorganization of Judaism.

For Ezekiel and his people, these years were bitter ones because the remnant of the Israelite domain, the little state of Judah, was eliminated by the rising Babylonian empire under Nebuchadrezzar (reigned 605–562 BC). Jerusalem surrendered in 597 BC. Israelite resistance was nevertheless renewed, and in 587–586 the city was destroyed after a lengthy siege. In both debacles, and indeed again in 582, large numbers from the best elements of the surviving population were forcibly deported to Babylonia.

Ezekiel prophesied that the exiles from both Judah and Israel would return to Palestine, leaving none in the Diaspora.

In the imminent new age, a new covenant would be made with the restored house of Israel, to whom Yahweh would give a new spirit and a new heart. The restoration would be an act of divine grace, for the sake of Yahweh's name.

Ezekiel's prophecies conclude with a vision of a restored Temple in Jerusalem. The Temple's form of worship would be re-established in Israel, and each of the ancient tribes would receive appropriate allotments of land. In contrast to those hoping for national restoration under a Davidic king, Ezekiel envisaged a theocratic community revolving around the Temple and its cult as the nexus of the restored Jewish state.

As other prophets have done before him, he sees the Yahweh-to-People relationship as analogous to that of a husband to unfaithful wife and therefore he understands the collapse of the life of Judah as a judgment for essential infidelity.

Ezekiel 38:1-13

Events will be in the end days. It is supposed enemies will come together to invade the land of Judea, and Yahweh will defeat them. Yahweh foresees who will be so, and lets them know by his word that he is against them; though they join together, the wicked shall not be unpunished.

Ezekiel 38:14-23

The enemy should make a formidable descent upon the land of Israel. When Israel dwell safely under the Divine protection, shalt not thou be made to know it by finding that endeavours to destroy them are made in vain? Promises of security are treasured up in the word of Yahweh, against the troubles and dangers.

In the destruction of the invaders, Yahweh shows that he is a great and holy Elohim. **(lookout for an alliance of Iran, Russia and other Arab nations against Israel.)**

Daniel

Daniel becomes recognised as a wise man in the Babylonian and Persian empires and has prophetic visions concerning Israel's future.

The prophet Daniel was taken captive during the Babylonian invasion of Jerusalem, in 607 BC.

Daniel became a chief minister at Nebuchadnezzar's royal court. He became known as a man who could interpret dreams and visions. Yahweh did miracles through Daniel that impressed King Nebuchadnezzar himself, so much so that he turned to the Jewish Elohim.

When the Medes and Persians conquered Babylon, King Cyrus ruled the Persian Empire.

He also had visions that Daniel had given interpretation to.

The great miracles mentioned in the Bible happened in the book of Daniel: the fiery furnace, the handwriting on the wall, and Daniel in the lion's den.

Daniel predicted the world governing empires before they came on the scene, first Babylon, second Persia, third Greece, fourth Rome, **and in the last days would be another Roman empire where the antichrist would arise.** At this time the Messiah will return and set up His everlasting kingdom. Daniel also predicted the exact day and year the Messiah would die. There is also a prophecy Daniel refers to as the 70th week, which speaks of a seven-year period in the future that will mark the second coming of the Messiah (Son of Man) coming with the clouds of heaven.

***** We are in that end time now. *****

Hosea

Hosea is instructed to marry a prostitute, who leaves him, and he must bring her back: a picture of Yahweh's relationship with us, Israel.

Hosea 6:1 "Come, let us return to Yahweh. For He has torn us, but He will heal us; He has wounded us, but He will bandage us".

Hosea 12:6 "Therefore, return to Yahweh your Elohim, Observe kindness and justice, And wait for your Elohim continually.

Hosea 14:1Return, O Israel, to Yahweh your Elohim, For you have stumbled because of your iniquity.

Hosea 14:2"Take words with you and return to Yahweh. Say to Him, "Take away all iniquity And receive us graciously, That we may present the fruit of our lips".

Joel

He is mentioned by name only once in the Hebrew Bible, in the introduction to that book, as the son of Pethuel (Joel 1:1). The name Joel combines the covenant name of Yahweh, YHWH (or Yahweh), and El (Yahweh), and has been translated as **"one to whom YHWH is Yahweh,"** that is, **a worshiper of YHWH.** Yahweh sends a plague of locusts to Judge Israel, but his judgment on the surrounding nations is coming, too.

No particular mention of Israel's sins is present in the book, but the consequences of the terrible events described are certainly clear:

***** Yahweh will one day wipe out all evil and start creation over. But through this destruction also comes eternal protection for those who believe in Him. *****

Salvation from the Messianic King is once again prophesied, but this time the Holy Spirit is prophesied to come too, causing seemingly ordinary people to have visions, divine dreams, and be filled with Yahweh's Spirit.

That's exactly what happened during Pentecost to Yeshua's disciples after His death and resurrection.

Joel 2:13 And rend your heart and not your garments " **Now return to Yahweh your Elohim**, For He is gracious and compassionate, slow to anger, abounding in loving kindness. And relenting of evil.

Amos

A shepherd named Amos preaches against the injustice of the Northern Kingdom of Israel.

The prophet Amos was born in the territory of Judah, but he prophesied to the northern kingdom of Israel and the wicked King Jeroboam II.

Amos prophesied against the nations around Israel and also condemned the northern kingdom of Israel for breaking Yahweh's laws.

He prophesied at the city of Bethel where King Jeroboam II resided, which had become a centre for idol worship.

He prophesied that the Israelites would be conquered by the Assyrians and removed from this place. *(as happened)*

Amos said that Yahweh could no more be in a relationship with the people of Israel that a man could be with an adulterous wife.

The prophet Amos focused his message of the chief cities in the northern kingdom, Bethel, the residence of the king and Samaria, the capital city.

These cities were greatly prosperous, they had been enlarged and were on the main trade routes. Amos directed his message on the wealthy who were robbing the poor, they were living in luxury in their sumptuous houses (Amos 3:15).

He likened their materialistic wives as "cows of Bashan" (Amos 4:1). They were gloating in all of their lusts and pomp and yet Yahweh saw what they were doing, for they were lacking justice, they had lost mercy, and they disregarded the poor.

They were careful to groom their shrines and altars, yet they had forgotten Yahweh and were given over to the most grotesque sorts of immorality, abuse, fornication, and drunkenness especially at the places of worship. Yahweh would not tolerate their ways and the prophet Amos came to announce the wrath of Yahweh.

Obadiah

The smallest Old Testament account, the Book of Obadiah is a vision written by Yahweh's prophet known as Obadiah, who prophesied against Israel's relative nation Edom.

Obadiah warns the neighbouring nation of Edom that they will be judged for plundering Jerusalem.

Obadiah is based on a prophetic vision concerning the fall of Edom, a mountain-dwelling nation whose founding father was Esau. Obadiah describes an encounter with Yahweh, who addresses Edom's arrogance and charges them for their violent actions against their brother nation, the House of Jacob (Israel)

Jonah

A disobedient prophet runs from Yahweh, is swallowed by a great fish, and then preaches Yahweh's message to the city of Nineveh.

Jonah received a calling from Yahweh to preach repentance to the people of Nineveh. Instead of obeying and going straight to Nineveh, he went to Joppa to board a ship to the city of Tarshish. Nineveh was inland from where Jonah lived and Tarshish was across the sea.

His disobedience brought punishment upon himself and others around him. After he boarded the ship to Tarshish there was a great storm. During the storm, the men working on the ship began calling upon their Yahwehs and idols to deliver them from whatever punishment was being given.

The workers found Jonah at the bottom of the ship asleep. They awakened him and asked him to pray to his Yahweh to protect them.

The men cast lots to see who had brought this punishment upon them (even though Jonah knew it was his fault). The lot fell upon Jonah. He confessed that he was a Hebrew and was running away from the Creator Yahweh. Jonah asked the men to throw him overboard. Instead, they tried harder to bring the ship to land. Jonah finally convinced them that he was the one who had brought judgment from Yahweh.

Perhaps Jonah thought that if he were dead then Yahweh would stop punishing the ones around him. The sailors agreed to throw him into the sea.

As soon as Jonah was tossed into the water the storm broke and everything was calm. The sailors probably had no idea what happened next.

Jonah was swallowed by a whale.

He was in the whale's belly for 3 days and 3 nights. **(is this three days and three nights prophetic)**

Jonah went into the water, but not to be killed by drowning. Instead, he was swallowed by a great fish (Yeshua called it a whale in Matthew 12:40). He was in the whale's belly for 3 days and 3 nights.

"Yeshua answered, 'Evil and sinful people are the ones who want to see a miracle for a sign. But no sign will be given to them, except the sign of the prophet Jonah'" (Matthew 12:39,).

What was the sign of Jonah? Yeshua goes on to explain: "For as Jonah was three days and three nights in the belly of the great fish, so will the Son of Man be three days and three nights in the heart of the earth" (Matthew 12:40).

Jonah awoke in the belly of the fish and cried out to Yahweh. He confessed his disobedience and told Yahweh that he would accomplish the task that Yahweh had called him to. Yahweh then instructed the whale to vomit Jonah out onto the dry ground.

Jonah lacks appreciation for Yahweh's mercy

After finding himself alive and on dry land, Jonah ran to the city of Nineveh. To his amazement, and apparent disappointment, the people of Nineveh did repent and asked for Yahweh's salvation. Yahweh knew that they needed a preacher to show them the error of their wickedness, but Jonah knew that Yahweh was merciful and would forgive them if they asked.

Even though Jonah preached to the people, he was not happy. He climbed to the top of a mountain to watch Yahweh destroy the city. Because of their repentance, Yahweh did not destroy them. Jonah complained again. To help teach Jonah a lesson, Yahweh caused a gourd to grow and to protect Jonah from the sun. A short time later Yahweh killed the gourd and Jonah became angry. Finally, Yahweh had Jonah's attention. Yahweh showed Jonah the foolishness of the fact that he was more concerned for the gourd than he was for the people.

The gourd, which had no soul, received more attention from the prophet Jonah than thousands of people who were destined to eternal punishment.

Micah

Micah confronts the leaders of Israel and Judah regarding their injustice, and prophecies that one day Yahweh himself will rule in perfect justice.

The book of Micah is a Prophetic Oracle. The prophet Micah wrote it 742-686 B.C. shortly before the Northern Kingdom's fall in 722 B.C. Key personalities are all the people of Samaria and Jerusalem.

The purpose of the book of Micah was to proclaim warning and judgment to both the Northern and the Southern Kingdoms. His message was similar to that of Isaiah and was written at about the same time. Micah described the impending judgment that would eventually exile the nation.

***** Then chapter five Micah miraculously predicts the birthplace of the Messiah in Bethlehem.**

Also in verse 2, he teaches that the Messiah is an infinite Savior, from everlasting, "But as for you, Bethlehem Ephrathah, too little to be among the clans of Judah.

From you, One will go forth for Me to be ruler in Israel. His goings forth are from long ago, from the days of eternity" (5:2).

*** In chapters 6-7, Micah declares what Yahweh requires of men, "He has told you, O man, what is good; **and what does Yahweh require of you but to do justice, to love kindness, and to walk humbly with your Elohim?"**

(6:8). Micah then proclaims Yahweh's restoration and salvation to His people, "Who is an Elohim like You, who pardons iniquity And passes over the rebellious act of the remnant of His possession? He does not retain His anger forever, because He delights in unchanging love"

Nahum

Nahum foretells of Yahweh's judgment on Nineveh, the capital of Assyria.

Habakkuk

Habakkuk pleads with Yahweh to stop the injustice and violence in Judah but is surprised to find that Yahweh will use the even more violent Babylonians to do so.

Zephaniah

Yahweh warns that he will judge Israel and the surrounding nations, but also that he will restore them in peace and justice.

Haggai

The people have abandoned the work of restoring Yahweh's temple in Jerusalem, and so Haggai takes them to the task.

Haggai was a prophet who, along with Zechariah, encouraged the returned exiles to rebuild the temple. His prophecies clearly show the consequences of disobedience. When people give priority to Yahweh and his house, they are blessed.

Zechariah

The prophet Zechariah calls Israel to return to Yahweh and records prophetic visions that show what's happening behind the scenes.

Zechariah 1:3 "Therefore say to them, 'Thus says the LORD of hosts, **"Return to Me," declares the LORD of hosts, "that I may return to you," says the LORD of hosts.**

Malachi

Malachi's mission was that of reinforcing his people's belief and confidence in Yahweh and reminding them of their responsibilities as members of the covenant community with Yahweh. Indeed the concept of the Covenant of Israel is fundamental to Malachi's message. It is a dominant theme in the book.

Malachi 3:7 "From the days of your fathers you have turned aside from My statutes and have not kept them **Return to Me, and I will return to you**," says the LORD of hosts. "But you say, 'How shall we return?'

The New Testament

The Q Gospel, comes from the German word Quelle, which means "source."

Many scholars conclude that Marks Gospel is a close copy of - **Homer's Odyssey**. – Written in 5th Century before Christian Era (BCE).

Also - **Hundreds of years before the supposed Jesus**, according to the Mithraic religion, (Mithraism)

Roman mystery religion Mithraism, also known as the Mithraic mysteries or the Cult of Mithras, was a Roman mystery religion cantered on the god Mithras. Although inspired by Iranian worship of the Zoroastrian divinity Mithra.

1) Three Wise Men of Persia came to visit the baby saviour-god Mithra, bringing him gifts of gold, myrrh and frankincense.

2) Mithra was born on December 25, "It was the **winter solstice** celebrated by ancients as the birthday of Mithraism's **sun god**".

3) According to Mithraism, before **Mithra died on a cross**, he celebrated a "Last Supper with his twelve disciples, who represented the twelve signs of the zodiac.

4) After the death of Mithra, his body was laid to rest in a rock tomb.

5) Mithra had a celibate priesthood.

6) Mithra ascended into heaven during the spring (Passover) equinox (the time when the sun crosses the equator making night and day of equal length).

It is clear Mark copied from Homer's Odyssey. Mark's Gospel of the New Testament although much was added later, returning to the ancient idol religion of Mithraism.

Is Christianity a re-branded version of more ancient Mithraic beliefs?

The New Testament is based on Marks Gospel with much added later.

There was no one called Jesus Christ.

Constantine's intention at Nicaea was to **create an entirely new god for his huge empire** who would unite all religious factions under one deity.

Presbyters were asked to debate and decide who their god would be.

Delegates argued among themselves, expressing personal motives for inclusion of writings that promoted the finer traits of their own special deity.

Throughout the meeting, howling factions were immersed in heated debates, and the names of 53 gods were tabled for discussion. "As of yet, no god had been selected by the council, and so they balloted to determine that matter.

For one year and five months the balloting lasted. . ." God's Book of Eskra, Prof. S.L. MacGuire's translation, Salisbury, 1922, chapter xlviii, paragraphs 36, 41. [Roman Catholic mix of legend and history] At the end of that time, Constantine returned to the gathering to discover that the presbyters had not agreed on a new deity, but had balloted down to a short list of five prospects: Caesar, Crishna [Krishna], Mithra, Horus, and Zeus [Roman Jupiter]. Historia Ecclesiastica, Eusebius, c. 325. Constantine was the ruling spirit at Nicaea, and he ultimately decided upon a new god for them. To involve British factions, he ruled that the name of the Druid god, "Hesus," be joined with the Eastern Saviour-god, Krishna (Krishna is Sanskrit for Christ), and thus "Hesus Krishna" [Jesus Christ] would be the official name of the New Roman god. A vote was taken, and it was with a majority show of hands (161 votes to 157) that both divinities become one God. Following long-standing heathen custom, Constantine used the official gathering and the Roman apotheosis decree to legally deify two deities as one and did so by democratic consent. **A new god was proclaimed and "officially" ratified by Constantine**. Acta Concilii Nicaeni, 1618.

However, despite these great Christian Deceptions including removing Yahweh's name from modern bibles and replacing it with Baal the name of the sun god. You can still of your own free will choose to be part of **Spiritual Israel** by accepting the **Spiritual God Yahweh**, who revealed His name to Moses and try to live by **His Ten Commandments**.

APPENDIX 1

Given the corruption of the so-called New Testament:

What can we be certain came from Yeshua's teachings?

1. **Shema – Hear Oh Israel. Yahweh our Elohim is One and is the only Elohim.** (I often supplement that as and is the only self-existent one. To give a better understanding that Yahweh is above and also through his creation, including us, with the potential to become His adopted children like Yeshua.

But not equal to Yahweh.

2. Keep Yahweh's commandments.

3. Keep Yahweh's appointed times as Leviticus 23 especially His Weekly Sabbath.

4. Love Yahweh our Elohim and all other people.

5. Love all people, not just your brothers and sisters.

6. Make peace not conflict.

7. Forgive without reservation or prejudice.

8. Do not judge others, especially with self-righteousness.

9. Be a servant to all others with spiritual happiness.

10. Listen to Yahweh's Holy Spirit, that's what Sabbath quiet time is for.

Apart from the substituted pagan names, I think you can reasonably take Revelations as pretty much uncorrupted. You can see the first of the five warning trumpets unfolding on the news programmes in climate change disasters.

It is challenging to keep Yahweh's Seventh Day Sabbath in this pagan world.

The principle is, you should do no work associated with earning a living.

You may host and lead family celebrations that bless family members and others.

You may do voluntary unpaid work that is helpful to others.

Although for some who struggle with health or caring issues, just acknowledging Yahweh and his Sabbath by praying at the beginning and end can suffice.

I struggle with ill health night and day. However, I still find time, especially at the beginning and end of Sabbaths to acknowledge Yahweh and His Sabbaths, even amidst all the medicines, inhalers and nebulisers.

APPENDIX 2

Keeping Yahweh's Sabbaths is ceasing from work and resting in Yahweh's presence.

1. Yahweh's Passover Lamb and Atonement for our sins is Messiah Yeshua.

2. Keeping the Passover is remembering that Yahweh brought our people out of Egypt and that Yeshua is our Passover lamb who bled for our sins and his sacrifice was accepted in his resurrection as the First Fruit of Creation and he is the **Shepherd of the gate to the eternal sheep flock**.

3. Keeping the Feast of Unleavened Bread and Yahweh's Torah is symbolic and proof of seeking righteous.

4. The receipt of Yahweh's Holy Spirit, Shavuot (Pentecost). Shavuot commemorates the anniversary of the day Yahweh gave the Commandments to Moses on Mount Sinai, and eventually the whole Torah to the Hebrew Nation.

5. The future Feast of trumpets heralding the return of King Yeshua ben David. (not long now)

6. The day of Atonement and Messiah Yeshua our personal Atonement.

7. The Feast of Sukkot or Tabernacles is looking forward to one thousand years of Messiah Yeshua King ben David's, who will establish the Kingdom and Torah of Yahweh across this planet earth with other first fruits resurrected or begotten by Yahweh.

8. The Last Great Day represents the resurrection of all the rest of humanity to the Day of Judgement and Decision.

APPENDIX 3

Word of warning, as you Keep Yahweh's Sabbaths, do not expect to see or hear visions or voices. It is about developing His inner Peace, a kind of mindfulness and that takes patience.

Matt 13: 31 – 43 He presented another parable to them, saying, "The kingdom of heaven is like a mustard seed, which a man took and sowed in his field; and this is smaller than all other seeds, but when it is full-grown, it is larger than the garden plants and becomes a tree, so that THE BIRDS OF THE AIR come and NEST IN ITS BRANCHES."

As you keep His Sabbaths, Yahweh's Holy Spirit slowly works in you.

Like the mustard seed, the Kingdom of Yahweh and His righteousness can slowly grow in you.

Final scripture:

Revelations 14:12 This calls for patient endurance on the part of the people of Yahweh who keep His commands and remain faithful to Messiah Yeshua.

ABOUT THE AUTHOR

Ernie Hasler started working as an apprentice engineer, in Scotland at the age of 16. He retired as a health and safety advisor after more than a half-century of work on some big jobs, also becoming the first advisor in Scotland to gain the specialist NEBOSH Diploma in environmental management.

Hasler became active in the trade union early in his career and saw many improvements in health and safety during his time. These important improvements stemmed from the Health and Safety at Work Act in 1974, which led to slow but significant increase in worker safety and welfare.

In his spare time, he ran a small charity, Plant Tree Save Planet, starting women's tree nurseries in poor countries, mostly funded by himself and his two sisters, however, he closed it when due to poor health and age he could not effectively check out recipients. He continues to fund tree planting through Trees for the Future, planting seedlings each year and helping poor families start agri-forestry farms. He has funded the planting of at least 100,000 trees and hopes to plant more before he dies, which won't be long now.

He has been a voluntary trustee with Emmaus Glasgow for twenty-four years, helping take it from an aspirational concept to a functioning community of up to twenty-seven previously homeless people.

75 years of experience has taught him that supporting people with needs on positive pathways is much more productive than punitive sanctions.

Photo of Hasler steering friends boat past the lair of the nuclear monster's base on the River Clyde.

Ernie is against nuclear weapons. They are a denial of our creative Elohim (God), and place belief and reliance on the biggest bully, the Alpha male.

A courageous and ingenious people would dig strong defensive positions all over the Highlands and train both men and women to make Scotland hard to invade.